A CHRISTMAS
ANTHOLOGY
OF
POETRY AND PAINTING

MADONNA AND CHILD WITH ANGELS
PIETRO DOMENICO DA MONTEPULCIANO
(*Early XVth Century*)

A Christmas Anthology of Poetry and Painting

Edited and Compiled by

VIVIAN CAMPBELL

with a Foreword by

WALTER PACH

Granger Poetry Library

GRANGER BOOK CO., INC.
Great Neck, N.Y.

First Published 1947
Reprinted 1979

International Standard Book Number
0-89609-181-3

Library of Congress Catalog Number
79-51963

Printed in the United States of America

FOREWORD

Among all peoples, and at all periods, there have been legends as to new birth in the world. Sometimes it is the sun god who comes back, after having disappeared in the winter; sometimes it is a flower goddess whose return is hailed with joy; sometimes a more spiritual sense in the stories identifies the new birth with a resurgence of goodness in the human race, a redemption from evil through a wiser, more generous vision.

All these elements are present in the great winter festival which we call Christmas, and which has its universal appeal precisely because it responds to very ancient needs in the nature of all mankind. Yet, certain features of the story—as it is retold in the poetry and pictures of this book—give to the old ideas a different and indeed a unique aspect. It is evidently one that is defined by the Christian religion, with its sources in the words of the Gospels. But we have seen that the Christian spirit goes back further in time and has a wider extent in space than the doctrines built upon the beautiful narrative. It is here given once more in the words of St. Luke, the text being accompanied by a reproduction of a page from the Gutenberg Bible—the first printing of the story, and so a landmark in history, for the invention of movable type permitted a limitless distribution of books. The present one recalls the earlier time when both the words in manuscript and the images drawn and painted by hand made of books a possession to be enjoyed only by a fortunate few.

Today we multiply not only the text but also the pictures. The great question, therefore, is as to their selection for, quite obviously, a book—if it is to be recommended—should contain only the really fine things; too many inferior ones have been produced, and are sold to people whose Christmas thinking is thus imposed upon, or even weakened.

It has, then, been with a double pleasure that I have gone through the pages compiled by Vivian Campbell. The first impression was of a work into which not one of the unworthy things had been permitted to enter, and then, more particularly, there was the delight of finding many of the finest of old friends here—and some new ones. My special interest being in pictures, and having seen so many of the originals reproduced in these pages, I am glad that acquaintance with them will be extended to people who may not previously have studied them. They will unquestionably be led to do so by the words through which great poets have described each scene for, as Miss Campbell so exactly observes, there is a striking correspondence between the thought of the writers and that of the sculptors, painters and other artists who illustrated the scenes described (as, for example, those who embroidered the English chasuble (page 30), who poured the enamel of that piece of Limoges (page 50) or who, in the XVIIth Century Holland, engraved the metal plate for "The Nativity" (page 72).

Sometimes, as with the image of "Spring" (page 16), we have the case of a contemporary re-interpretation, for that great master Pieter Brueghel had around him a whole group of fine engravers to make his drawings accessible to the thousands of people who could not own an original. Since he was unable, evidently, to produce enough original drawings for them, the means of reaching the wider public was provided by able craftsmen, artists in their own medium. The present book will carry on that work again. If the modern processes of reproduction lose something of the incisive impression of a Brueghel print, they make up for that by the accuracy with which they render, within such small space, the mighty impressions of a life-size sculpture by Michelangelo (page 62). May I suggest that here the reader turn to pages 51 and 53 and read again the glorious poems of John Milton, for when we confront the style of the great Italian with that of the great Englishman, we see that the two artists meet not only in celebrating the beauty of the Christmas story, but in showing how it inspired their rising to the most august heights of art.

Perhaps it will seem contradictory if I say I am glad that the main body of the book does not take us to those lofty regions. When there, Michelangelo and John Milton remain human and, had they failed to do so, even they could not fittingly be included in these pages. For, as I have already affirmed, the Christmas story is so widely loved because it is so human. The young mother, the "smiling babe" sung of by William Blake (page 29); the group of the two with saints as seen in the image by a contemporary of the supremely great Cimabue (page 66); the "Winter in the Country" (page 44) painted at nearly our own time and by one of our own people, Fanny Palmer (a new-found friend); and again the Mother and Child (page 74) portrayed by another woman, Kaethe Kollwitz, the nobly human artist of modern Germany—do not all these words and pictures appeal to everyone, everywhere, when there is acceptance of the spirit which asked for peace on earth, good will to men?

—WALTER PACH

6

FOR MY MOTHER

ACKNOWLEDGMENTS

We are grateful to the publishers indicated below for the use of two poems not in the public domain:

"The Starlight Night," page 47, is reprinted from *Poems* by Gerard Manley Hopkins, with the permission of the Oxford University Press and the courtesy of the poet's family.

"Little Jesus," page 75, is reprinted, by permission, from the Modern Library edition of *Francis Thompson's Poems,* Random House, Inc.

CONTENTS

A Selection of Christmas Carols

LIST OF ILLUSTRATIONS
AND ACKNOWLEDGMENTS

11

INTRODUCTION

The poems and works of art in this anthology have been chosen from among the countless personal interpretations given, throughout the centuries, to the Christmas Story.

In order to enhance the individuality of these works, I have placed a particular painting or piece of sculpture beside that poem which, to me, similarly described a day so close to us all. While, in a few instances, it is merely the technical structure which makes for the choice of companionpiece, the reason for selection is more often the manner of expression. It is hard to believe, for example, that the writer of "Gloria in Excelsis" was not the sculptor of the two smiling angels who face the poem. Or that Brueghel did not write "Preparations".

Man's humility in the face of true beauty, to be found on every page, is equaled only by the variety of the artists' approaches to this timeless theme. Here are the lullaby, the drinking song, the elegy, the narrative and the ode; and, opposite each, a work of art which could have been executed expressly to illustrate it.

I am greatly indebted to those who read this book while in preparation, and to those museums and galleries who so kindly granted me permission to reproduce certain of the works in their collections. Lastly, I should like to express my gratitude to the publishers and printers of this volume for the complete understanding which has gone into its production and workmanship.

—Vivian Campbell

Ucas sirus· natione anthi
ocensis· arte medic° · disci
pulus apostolox· postea
paulū secut° usq3 ad con
fessione ex serviens dño sine crimine:
nam neq3 uxorem unq3 habuit neq3 fi
lios:septuaginta et quatuor annorū
obijt in bithinia· plen° spiritu sancto.
Qui cū iam scripta essent euāgelia · p
matheū quide in iudea· p marcū aut
in italia:sancto instigante spiritu in
achaie partibz hpc scripsit euangeliū:
significans etiā ipe in principio ante
suū alia esse descripta · Cui extra ea q
ordo euāgelice dispositionis exposci
ta maxime necessitas laboris fuit:ut
primū grecis fidelibz omni pphetati
one venturi in carne dei cristi manife
stata humanitate ne iudaicis fabulis
attenti : in solo legis desiderio teneā
tur : uel ne hereticis fabulis et stultis
solicitationibz seducti recciderent a ve
ritate elaboraret:dehinc·ut in princi
pio euangelij iohānis natiuitate pre
sumpta·cui euangelium scriberet et in
quo elect° scriberet indicaret: potestās i
se cōpleta esse·q essent ab alijs incspa
ta · Cui ideo post baptismū filij dei a
pfectione generatōnis i cristo implere
repetēde a pricipio natiuitatis huma
ne potestas pmissa e : ut requirentibz
demonstraret in quo apprehendēs e
rat per nathan filiū dauid introitu re
currentis i dru generationis admisso·
indisparabilis dei pdicās in homini
bus cristū suū·pfecti opus hois redire
in se p filiū faceret:qui per dauid patrē
venientibus iter pbebat in cristo. Cui
luce non immerico etiā scribēdorum
actuū apostolox potestas i ministerio
datur:ut deo in dru pleno et filio pdi
ctionis extincto· oratione ab apostolis

facta · sorte domini electionis numer°
compleretur : sicq3 paulus cōsumma
tione apostolicis actibz daret·quē diu
cōtra stimulū recalcitrante dñs elegis
set. Quod et legentibz ac requirentibz
deū · et si per singula expediri a nobis
utile fuerat:scietis tame q operātem
agricolā oporteat de suis fructibus e
dere · vitauim° publicā curiositatem:
ne nō tā volentibz deū demōstrare vide
remur·quā fastidientibus prodidisse.

Alius prologus

Quoniā quide multi cona
ti sūt ordinare nar
ratones q i nobis com
plete sūt rex·sicut tradi
derūt nobis q ab inicio
ipi viderūt · et ministri
fuerūt sermonis:visū e et michi assecuto
oīa a pricipio diligēter ex ordie tibi
scribere optie theophile : ut cognoscas
eox verbox de qbz erudit° es veritate. cū l.

Uit in diebus herodis re
gis iudee sacerdos quidam
nomine zacharias de vi
ce abia·et uxor illi de filia
bus aaron : et nomen eius elizabeth.
Erant autem iusti ambo ante deum:
incedentes in omnibus mandatis z
iustificationibus domini sine quere
la · Et non erat illis filius · eo q es
set elizabeth sterilis:et ambo proces
sissent i diebz suis. Factū est aūt cū sa
cerdotio fungeretur zacharias in ordi
ne vicis sue ante deū : scdm cōsuetudi
nem sacerdotij sorte exijt ut incensum
poneret ingressus in templū domini.
Et omnis multitudo ipli erat orās fo
ris hora incensi. Apparuit autem illi
angelus dñi:stans a dextris altaris

THE BEGINNING OF THE CHRISTMAS STORY

FROM THE GUTENBERG BIBLE

(About 1455)

AND THERE WERE SHEPHERDS

And there were shepherds in the same country abiding in the field, and keeping watch by night over their flock. And an angel of the Lord stood by them, and the glory of the Lord shone round about them: and they were sore afraid. And the angel said unto them, Be not afraid; for behold, I bring you good tidings of great joy which shall be to all the people. For there is born to you this day in the city of David a Saviour, who is Christ the Lord. And this is the sign unto you: Ye shall find a babe wrapped in swaddling clothes, and lying in a manger. And suddenly there was with the angel a multitude of the heavenly host praising God, and saying:

Glory to God in the highest,
And on earth peace among men
in whom he is well pleased.

And it came to pass, when the angels went away from them into heaven, the shepherds said one to another, Let us now go even unto Bethlehem, and see this thing that is come to pass, which the Lord hath made known unto us.

And they came with haste, and found both Mary and Joseph, and the babe lying in the manger. And when they saw it, they made known concerning the saying which was spoken to them about this child. And all that heard it wondered at the things which were spoken unto them by the shepherds. But Mary kept all these sayings, pondering them in her heart. And the shepherds returned, glorifying and praising God for all the things that they had heard and seen, even as it was spoken unto them.

—St. Luke II: 8-21
(American Revised Version)

SPRING

PIETER BRUEGHEL THE ELDER

(1525-1569)

PREPARATIONS

Yet if His Majesty, our sovereign lord,
  Should of His own accord
Friendly Himself invite,
And say, "I'll be your guest tomorrow night,"
How should we stir ourselves, call and command
All hands to work! "Let no man idle stand!

"Set me fine Spanish tables in the hall;
See they be fitted all;
Let there be room to eat
And order taken that there want no meat.
See every sconce and candlestick made bright,
That without tapers they may give a light.

"Look to the presence: are the carpets spread,
The dazie o'er the head,
The cushions in the chairs,
And all the candles lighted on the stairs?
Perfume the chambers, and in any case
Let each man give attendance in his place!"

Thus, if a king were coming, would we do;
And 'twere good reason too;
For 'tis a duteous thing
To show all honor to an earthly king,
And after all our travail and our cost,
So he be pleased, to think no labor lost.

But at the coming of the King of Heaven
All's set at six and seven;
We wallow in our sin,
Christ cannot find a chamber in the inn.
We entertain Him always like a stranger,
And, as at first, still lodge Him in the manger.

—ANONYMOUS
    (*Christ Church Mss.*)

17

VIRGIN AND CHILD
FRENCH
(*About 1400*)

CAROL

I sing of a maiden
That is matchless;
King of all kings
To her Son she chose.

He came all so still
There His mother was,
As dew in April
That falleth on the grass.

He came all so still
To His mother's bower,
As dew in April
That falleth on the flower.

He came all so still
There His mother lay,
As dew in April
That falleth on the spray.

Mother and maiden
Was never none but she;
Well may such a lady
Godde's mother be.

—ANONYMOUS
(XVth Century)

THE NATIVITY
BOOK OF HOURS, FRANCO-FLEMISH
(*Late XVth Century*)

THIS IS THE DAY WHICH GOD HATH MADE

Then Joseph rose up and brought an ass, and he set Mary upon it, and they went to Bethlehem. And there followed him on the road a priest whose name was Samuel, and he went with them. And when they had come a distance of about three stadia, Joseph turned and looked at Mary and saw that she was smiling and laughing, and she said unto him, "Behold, birth pangs have seized upon me, for I have drawn nigh to my time of bringing forth." And Joseph said unto her, "Where shall I put thee in this place?"

And then Joseph lifted up his eyes and saw a cave and he brought Mary into that cave and went forth to seek for a midwife for her. And as he was going along the road, behold, he saw the earth trembling. And again, he saw oxen feeding, and they lifted up their eyes to heaven. And again, he saw a great river wherein were many sheep, and they wished to drink, but only lifted up their eyes to heaven. And then Joseph lifted up his eyes toward the mountains of Bethlehem, and he saw a woman coming, and he came to her and saluted her. And that woman said unto him, "Whither goest thou, and what dost thou want?" And Joseph said unto her, "I want a midwife." And that woman said unto him, "Who is this woman who is about to bring forth in the cave?" And Joseph said unto her, "It is Mary, who is with child by the Holy Spirit." And that woman said, "Dost thou believe what thou sayest?" And Joseph said, "Come to her"; and the two of them went together into the cave.

And they saw a cloud of light which crowned Mary, and also there went forth from the inside of the cave a great light, and it shone in all that land; and they saw a child lying in a manger. And at that moment the woman cried out with a loud voice and said, "My soul doth magnify the Lord this day, because I have seen a new light and great glory. That Child who hath been born this day is the God of Israel, and He shall deliver His people from their sins."

(Translated by E. A. Wallis Budge from the Ethiopic Manuscripts)

VIRGIN AND CHILD WITH ANGELS
SCHOOL OF CAMPIN
(*XVth Century*)

CRADLE SONG

O my deir hert, young Jesus sweit,
    Prepare Thy creddil in my spreit,
And I sall rock Thee in my hert
And never mair from Thee depart.

But I sall praise Thee evermoir
With sangis sweit unto Thy gloir;
The knees of my hert sall I bow,
And sing that richt *Balulalow!*

—ANONYMOUS
(XVIth Century)

ADORATION OF THE SHEPHERDS
Albrecht Altdorfer
(XVIth Century)

OUR LADY'S SONG

Iesu, swete Sone dere!
  On porful bed list Thou here,
And that me greveth sore;
For Thi cradel is ase a bere,
Oxe and asse beth Thi fere:
  Weepe ich mai tharfore.

Iesu, swete, beo noth wroth,
Thou ich nabbe clout ne cloth
  The on for to folde,
  The on to folde ne to wrappe,
For ich nabble clout ne lappe;
Bote ley Thou Thi fet to my pappe,
  And wite The from the colde.

—Anonymous
(about 1375)

25

MADONNA AND CHILD WITH ANGELS

HANS MEMLING

(1435-1494)

A LULLING, OR CRADLE SONG

Sweet was the song the Virgin sang
    When she to Bethlehem Iuda came:
And was delivered of a Son,
    That blessed Jesus hath to name.
        Lulla, lulla, lulla, lullaby,
Lulla, lulla, lulla, lullaby, sweet Babe, sung she,
    My Son and too a Saviour born,
Who hast vouchsaféd from on high
    To visit us that were forlorn;
La lula, la lula, la lullaby, sweet Babe, sung she,
And rocked Him sweetly on her knee.

—WILLIAM BALLET's Lute Book
(XVIth Century)

MADONNA AND CHILD
ANDREA DEL VEROCCHIO
(1435-1488)

A CRADLE SONG

Sweet dreams, for a shade
  O'er my lovely infant's head;
Sweet dreams of pleasant streams
By happy, silent, moony beams.

Sweet sleep, with soft down
Weave thy brows and infant crown.
Sweet sleep, Angel mild,
Hover o'er my happy child.

Sweet smiles, in the night
Hover over my delight;
Sweet smiles, mother's smiles,
All the livelong night beguiles.

Sweet moans, dovelike sighs,
Chase not slumber from thy eyes.
Sweet moans, sweeter smiles,
All the dovelike moans beguiles.

Sleep, sleep, happy child,
All creation slept and smil'd;
Sleep, sleep, happy sleep,
While o'er thee thy mother weep.

Sweet babe, in thy face
Holy image I can trace.
Sweet babe, once like thee,
Thy Maker lay and wept for me,

Wept for me, for thee, for all,
When He was an infant small.
Thou His image ever see,
Heavenly face that smiles on thee,

Smiles on thee, on me, on all;
Who became an infant small.
Infant smiles are His own smiles;
Heaven and earth to peace beguiles.

—William Blake
(1757-1827)

ADORATION OF THE MAGI
EMBROIDERED CHASUBLE, ENGLISH
(Mid XIVth Century)

From: THE SHEPHERD'S HYMN

To Thee, meek Majesty, soft King
  Of simple graces and sweet loves!
Each of us his lamb will bring,
  Each his pair of silver doves!
At last, in fire of Thy fair eyes,
Ourselves become our own best sacrifice!

—RICHARD CRASHAW
(1613-1649)

MADONNA AND CHILD WITH ANGELS
CENTRAL ITALIAN SCHOOL
(*XIIIth Century—About 1250*)

From: A HYMN OF THE NATIVITY

Welcome to our wondering sight,
 Eternity shut in a span!
Summer in winter! Day in night!
 Heaven in earth! and God in man!
Great little One, whose glorious birth
 Lifts earth to Heaven, stoops Heaven to earth.

     —RICHARD CRASHAW
     (1613-1649)

MADONNA AND CHILD
BOOK OF HOURS, FRANCO-FLEMISH
(*Late XVth Century*)

THE SHEPHERD'S SONG

"O than the fairest day thrice fairer night!
    Night to best day in which a sun doth rise
Of which that golden eye, which clears the skies,
    Is but a sparkling ray, a shadow light.
And blessed ye, in silly pastors' sight,
    Mild creatures, in whose warm crib now lies
That heav'n sent Youngling, holy maid born wight,*
    Midst, end, beginning of our prophecies.
Blest cottage that hath flow'rs in winter spread,
    Though wither'd—blessed grass, that hath the grace
To deck, and be a carpet to that place."
    Thus sang, unto the sounds of oaten reed,
Before the Babe, the shepherds bow'd on knees;
    And springs ran nectar, honey dropped from trees.

—WILLIAM DRUMMOND
(1589-1649)

---

* brave.

VIRGIN AND CHILD, ST. ANNE AND ST. AFRA
AUGSBURG SCHOOL, GERMAN
(*About 1510-1520*)

KING ARTHUR'S WAES-HAEL

Waes-hael for knight and dame!
    O merry be their dole!
Drink-hael! In Jesu's name
    We fill the tawny bowl:
But cover down the curving crest,
Mould of the Orient Lady's breast.

Waes-hael! yet lift no lid:
    Drain ye the reeds for wind.
Drink-hael! the milk was hid
    That soothed that Babe divine;
Hush'd, as this hollow channel flows,
He drew the balsam from the rose.

Waes-hael! thus glow'd the breast
    Where a God yearn'd to cling;
Drink-hael! So Jesu press'd
    Life from its mystic spring;
Then hush and bend in reverent sign
And breathe the thrilling reeds for wine.

Waes-hael! in shadowy scene
    Lo! Christmas children we:
Drink-hael! behold we lean
    At a far Mother's knee;
To dream that thus her bosom smiled,
And learn the lip of Bethlehem's Child.

—ROBERT HAWKER
(1804-1875)

THE ADORATION OF THE MAGI
Giovanni Baronzio
(Mid XIVth Century)

From: OF THE BIRTH OF OUR SAVIOUR

In numbers, and but these few,
  I sing Thy birth, O Jesu.
Thou pretty Baby, born here
With superabundant scorn here:
Who for Thy princely port here,
  Hadst, for Thy place
  Of birth, a base
Out-stable for Thy court here.

Instead of neat enclosures
Of interwoven osiers,
Instead of fragrant posies
O daffodils and roses,
Thy cradle, kingly Stranger,
  As gospel tells,
  Was nothing else
But here a homely manger.

But we with silks not crewels,
With sundry precious jewels,
And lily-work will dress Thee;
And, as we dispossess Thee
Of clouts, we'll make a chamber,
  Sweet Babe, for Thee
  Of ivory,
And plaster'd round with amber.

—ROBERT HERRICK
(1591-1674)

THE ADORATION OF THE MAGI
ILLUMINATED MANUSCRIPT, FLEMISH
(XVth Century)

TO HIS SAVIOUR, A CHILD

Go, pretty child, and bear this flower
    Unto thy little Saviour.
And tell Him, by that bud now blown,
He is the Rose of Sharon known.
When thou hast said so, stick it there
Upon His bib, or stomacher.
And tell Him, for good handsell too,
That thou hast brought a whistle new,
Made of a clean straight oaten reed,
To charm His cries at time of need.
Tell Him, for coral, thou hast none;
But if thou hadst, He should have one.
But poor thou art, and known to be
Even as moneyless as He.
Lastly, if thou canst, win a kiss
From those mellifluous lips of His,
Then never take a second on
To spoil the first impression.

—ROBERT HERRICK
(1591-1674)

MADONNA AND CHILD WITH ANGELS
MASTER OF THE JARVES CASSONI
(*About 1450*)

WHAT SWEETER MUSIC

What sweeter music can we bring
  Than a carol for to sing
The birth of this our heavenly King?
Awake the voice! awake the string!
Heart, ear, and eye, and every thing.
Awake! the while the active finger
Runs division with the singer.

Dark and dull night, fly hence away,
And give the honor to this day
That sees December turned to May.

If we ask the reason, say
The why and wherefore all things here
Seem like the springtime of the year.

Why does 'the chilling winter morn
Smile like a field beset with corn,
Or smell like to a mead new shorn,
Thus on the sudden? Come and see
The cause why things thus fragrant be:
'Tis He is born, whose quick'ning birth
Gives life and luster, public mirth
To heaven, and the under earth.

We see Him come, and know Him ours,
Who with His sunshine and His showers
Turns all the patient ground to flowers.

The Darling of the world is come,
And fit it is we find a room
To welcome Him. The nobler part
Of all the house here is the heart,
Which we will give Him, and bequeath
This holly and this ivy wreath,
To do Him honor, who's our King,
And Lord of all this revelling.

—ROBERT HERRICK
(1591-1674)

43

SIGNS OF CHRISTMAS

When on the barn's thatch'd roof is seen
    The moss in tufts of liveliest green;
When Roger to the woodpile goes,
And, as he turns, his fingers blows;
When all around is cold and drear,
Be sure that Christmastide is near.

When up the garden walk in vain
We seek for Flora's lovely train;
When the sweet hawthorn bower is bare,
And bleak and cheerless is the air;
When all seems desolate around,
Christmas advances o'er the ground.

When Tom at eve comes home from plough,
And brings the mistletoe's green bough,
With milk-white berries spotted o'er,
And shakes it the sly maids before,
Then hangs the trophy up on high,
Be sure that Christmastide is nigh.

When Hal, the woodman, in his clogs
Brings home the huge unwieldy logs,
That, hissing on the smould'ring fire,
Flame out at last a quivering spire;
When in his hat the holly stands,
Old Christmas musters up his bands.

When, clustered round the fire at night,
Old William talks of ghost and sprite,
And, as a distant outhouse gate
Slams by the wind, they fearful wait,
While some each shadowy nook explore,
Then Christmas pauses at the door.

When Dick comes shiv'ring from the yard,
And says, "The pond is frozen hard,"
While from his cap, all white with snow,
The moisture trickling drops below;
While carols sound, the night to cheer,
Then Christmas and his train are here.

—WILLIAM HONE's Year Book, 1832

MADONNA AND CHILD WITH SAINTS
Giovanni di Paolo
(1403-1482)

THE STARLIGHT NIGHT

Look at the stars! Look, look up at the skies!
   O look at all the fire-folk sitting in the air!
  The bright boroughs, the circle-citadels there!
Down in dim woods the diamond delves! the elves'-eyes!
The grey lawns cold where gold, where quickgold lies!
  Wind-beat whitebeam! airy abeles set on a flare!
  Flake-doves sent floating forth at a farmyard scare!—
Ah well! it is all a purchase, all is.a prize.

Buy then! bid then!—What?—Prayer, patience, alms, vows.
Look, look: a May-mess, like on orchard boughs!
  Look! March-bloom, like on mealed-with-yellow sallows!
These are indeed the barn; within doors house
The shocks. This piece-bright paling shuts the spouse
  Christ home, Christ and His mother and all His hallows.

—GERARD MANLEY HOPKINS
(1844-1889)

ADORING ANGEL
MANNER OF ANTONIO ROSSELLINO, ITALIAN
(*XVth Century*)

A HYMN ON THE NATIVITY OF MY SAVIOUR

I sing the birth was born tonight,
    The Author both of life and light.
  The angels so did sound it.
And like the ravish'd shepherds said,
Who saw the light and were afraid,
    Yet search'd and true they found it.

The Son of God, th' eternal King,
That did us all salvation bring,
    And freed the soul from danger,
He whom the whole world could not take,
The word, which heaven and earth did make,
    Was now laid in a manger.

The Father's wisdom willed it so,
The Son's obedience knew no *no,*
    Both wills were in one stature;
And, as that wisdom had decreed,
The word was now made flesh indeed,
    And took on Him our nature.

What comfort by Him do we win,
Who made Himself the price of sin,
    To make us heirs of glory!
To see this Babe all innocence,
A Martyr born in our defence,
    Can man forget the story?

—BEN JONSON
(1573-1637)

49

ADORATION OF THE SHEPHERDS
LIMOGES ENAMEL, FRENCH
(*Early XVIth Century*)

ODE ON THE MORNING OF CHRIST'S NATIVITY

This is the month and this the happy morn,
 Wherein the Son of Heaven's eternal King,
Of wedded maid and virgin mother born,
Our great redemption from above did bring;
For so the holy sages once did sing
 That He our deadly forfeit should release,
And with His Father work us a perpetual peace.

—JOHN MILTON
(1608-1674)

ADORATION OF THE SHEPHERDS
BARTOLO DI FREDI
(1330-1410)

HYMN

It was the winter wild
  While the heaven-born Child
All meanly wrapt in the rude manger lies.
  Nature in awe to Him
  Had doff'd her gaudy brim
With her great Master so to sympathize:
  It was no season then for her
  To wanton with the sun, her lusty paramour.

—John Milton
(1608-1674)

FOR CHRISTMAS MORNING

Fairest of morning lights appear,
   Thou blest and gaudy day,
On which was born our Saviour dear
   Arise and come away.

See, see our pensive breasts do pant,
   Like gasping land we lie;
The holy dews our souls do want,
   We faint, we pine, we die.

Let from the skies a joyful rain,
   Like`meal or manna, fall;
Whose searching drops our sins may drain,
   And quench our sorrows all.

This day prevents His day of doom,
   His mercy now is nigh;
The mighty God of love is come,
   The Dayspring from on high.

Behold the great Creator makes
   Himself an house of clay;
A robe of virgin-flesh He takes,
   Which He will wear for ay.

Hark, hark, the wise eternal word,
   Like a weak infant cries,
In form of servant is the Lord,
   And God in cradle lies.

This wonder struck the world amazed,
   It shook the starry frame;
Squadrons of spirits stood and gazed,
   Then down in troops they came.

Glad shepherds ran to view this sight,
   A choir of angels sings,
And Eastern sages with delight
   Adore this King of kings.

Join then, all hearts that are not stone,
   And all our voices prove,
To celebrate this Holy One,
   The God of peace and love.

—THOMAS PESTEL *(1659)*

ADORATION OF THE KINGS

GERMAN PSALTER

(*XIIIth Century, about 1250*)

From: CHRISTMAS IN THE OLDEN TIME

Heap on more wood! The wind is chill;
But let it whistle as it will,
We'll keep our Christmas merry still.
Each age has deem'd the new-born year
The fittest time for festal cheer.

On Christmas Eve the bells were rung;
On Christmas Eve the Mass was sung.
That only night in all the year
Saw the stoled priest the chalice rear.
The damsel donn'd her kirtle sheen,
The hall was dress'd with holly green.
Forth to the wood did merry men go
To gather in the mistletoe.

Then came the merry masquers in,
And carols roar'd with blithesome din.
If unmelodious was the song,
It was a hearty note, and strong.
But O! what masquers, richly dight,
Can boast of bosoms half so light?
England was merry England when
Old Christmas brought his sports again.
'Twas Christmas broach'd the mightiest ale;
'Twas Christmas told the merriest tale;
A Christmas gambol oft could cheer
The poor man's heart through half the year.

—Sir Walter Scott
(1771-1832)

THE NATIVITY WITH ST. JEROME
Girolamo di Benvenuto
(XVth Century)

MARCELLUS SPEAKS

Some say that ever 'gainst that season comes
Wherein our Saviour's birth is celebrated,
The bird of dawning singeth all night long:
And then, they say, no spirit can walk abroad;
The nights are wholesome; then no planets strike,
No fairy takes, nor witch has power to charm;
So hallow'd and so gracious is the time.

—WILLIAM SHAKESPEARE (1564-1616)
From Hamlet, *Act I, Scene 1*

ST. ANNE ENTHRONED WITH VIRGIN AND CHILD

CASTILIAN

(*Late XVth Century*)

YE GREATE ASTONISHMENT

Whosoever on ye nighte of ye nativity of ye young Lord Jesus, in ye great snows, shall fare forth bearing a succulent bone for ye loste and lamenting hounde, a wisp of hay for ye shivering horse, a cloak of warm raiment for ye stranded wayfarer, a bundle of fagots for ye twittering crone, a flagon of red wine for him whose marrow withers, a garland of bright berries for one who has worn chains, gay arias of lute and harp for all huddled birds who thought that song was dead, and divers lush sweetmeats for such babes' faces as peer from lonely windows—

To him shall be proffered and returned gifts of such an astonishment as will rival the hues of the peacock and the harmonies of heaven, so that though he live to ye greate age when man goes stooping and querulous because of the nothing that is left in him, yet shall he walk upright and remembering, as one whose heart shines like a great star in his breaste.

—Source Unknown

MADONNA AND CHILD
MICHELANGELO
(1475-1564)

PATREM PARIT FILIA

Behold the father is his daughter's son.
 The bird that built the nest is hatched therein,
The old of years an hour hath not out run.
Eternal life to live doth now begin.
The word is dumb—the mirth of heaven doth weep,
Might feeble is, and force doth faintly creep.

—ROBERT SOUTHWELL
(1560-1593)

THE ADORATION OF THE MAGI
BENVENUTO DI GIOVANNI
(*1436-1518*)

NEW PRINCE, NEW POMP

Behold a sely tender Babe
   In freezing winter night
In homely manger trembling lies,
   Alas, a piteous sight.

The inns are full, no man will yield
   This little Pilgrim bed;
But forced He is with sely beasts
   In crib to shroud His head.

Despise not Him for lying there,
   First what He is inquire;
An orient pearl is often found
   In depth of dirty mire.

Weigh not His crib, His wooden dish,
   Nor beasts that by Him feed;
Weigh not His mother's poor attire,
   Nor Joseph's simple weed.

This stable is a Prince's court,
   The crib His chair of state;
The beasts are parcel of His pomp,
   The wooden dish His plate.

The parsons in that poor attire
   His royal liveries wear;
The Prince Himself is come from heaven,
   This pomp is prizéd there.

With joy approach, O Christian wight,
   Do homage to thy King;
And highly prize His humble pomp,
   Which He from heaven doth bring.

—ROBERT SOUTHWELL
(1560-1593)

MADONNA AND CHILD WITH SAINTS
CONTEMPORARY OF CIMABUE
(*XIIIth Century*)

From: A CRADLE HYMN

See the kinder shepherds round Him,
  Telling wonders from the sky!
Where they sought Him, there they found Him,
  With His virgin mother by.

See the lovely babe a-dressing;
  Lovely infant, how He smiled!
When He wept, the mother's blessing
  Soothed and hush'd the Holy Child.

Lo, He slumbers in His manger,
  Where the horned oxen fed:
Peace, my darling, here's no danger,
  Here's no ox anear thy bed.

—Isaac Watts
(1674-1748)

ANGELS
NORTH ITALIAN
(*Late XVth or Early XVIth Century*)

GLORIA IN EXCELSIS

The angels sung, and thus sing we,
   "To God on high all glory be.
Let Him on earth His peace bestow,
And unto men His favor show."

—George Wither
(1588-1667)

MADONNA ENTHRONED WITH ANGELS
PROVINCIAL FOLLOWER OF PIERO DELLA FRANCESCA
(*About 1450*)

LET US SING OUR ROUNDELAYS

So now is come our joyful'st feast;
  Let every man be jolly.
Each room with ivy-leaves is dressed,
And every post with holly.
    Though some churls at our mirth repine
    Round your foreheads garlands twine,
    Drown sorrow in a cup of wine,
And let us all be merry.

Now all our neighbours' chimneys smoke,
And Christmas blocks are burning;
The ovens they with baked meats choke,
And all their spits are turning.
    Without the door let sorrow lie,
    And if for cold it hap to die,
    We'll bury't in a Christmas pie,
And evermore be merry.

Now every lad is wondrous trim,
And no man minds his labour;
Our lasses have provided them
A bagpipe and a tabor.
    Young men, and maids, and girls and boys,
    Give life to one another's joys,
    And you anon shall by their noise

Perceive that they are merry.
Then wherefore in these merry days
Should we, I pray, be duller?
No; let us sing our roundelays
To make our mirth the fuller.
    And, whilst thus inspired we sing,
    Let all the streets with echoes ring;
    Woods, and hills, and everything,
Bear witness we are merry.

GEORGE WITHER.
(1588-1667)

THE NATIVITY
F. H. Van Hoven
(*XVIIth Century*)

A CHRISTMAS CAROL

Cognovit bos et asinus
quod puer erat dominus.

On Twelfth-Day morn, old Christmas Day,
Ere midnight scarce be past away,
'Tis by our countryfold averr'd,
And let no scoffer doubt their word,
That, oft as Yuletime wheeleth round,
The bees in hive, by weather bound,
Hum, only on this night, for mirth,
In worship of our Saviour's birth.
That, as aforetime, even now
Both ox and ass before Him bow;
That, in remembrance of that dawn,
When unto herdsmen on the lawn
Good news was by an angel told,
The sheep, confined within the fold,
Face eastward, while their kin without
Gang in procession round about.
That on this night the forester sees
The deer a-falling on their knees.
That now, for once in all the year,
Our chapel-clerk, Sir Chanticleer,
Incessantly will sing and say
His nocturnes on till prime of day,
And, in observant wise, prolong
His lauds, and merry matin-song.
Witness of plants. The rose, in time
To bloom at sound of Christmas chime.
And, though the earth be draped with snow,
And Boreas ne'er so chilly blow,
Saint Joseph's Glastonbury Thorn,
That yearly flowers on Yuleday morn.

—GEORGE RATCLIFFE WOODWARD
(1848)

MOTHER AND CHILD
KAETHE KOLLWITZ
(*1867-1945*)

LITTLE JESUS

*Ex ore infantium, Deus, et lactenium
perfecisti laudem*

Little Jesus, wast Thou shy
      Once, and just so small as I?
And what did it feel like to be
Out of Heaven, and just like me?
Didst Thou sometimes think of *there,*
And ask where all the angels were?
I should think that I would cry
For my house all made of sky;
I would look about the air,
And wonder where the angels were;
And at waking 'twould distress me—
Not an angel there to dress me!
Hadst Thou ever any toys,
Like us little girls and boys?
And didst Thou play in Heaven with all
The angels that were not too tall,
With stars for marbles? Did the things
Play *Can you see me?* through their wings?
And did Thy Mother let Thee spoil
Thy robes, with playing on *our* soil?
How nice to have them always new
In Heaven, because 'twas quite clean blue!

Didst Thou kneel at night to pray,
And didst Thou join Thy hands, this way?
And did they tire sometimes, being young,
And make the prayer seem very long?
And dost Thou like it best, that we
Should join our hands to pray to Thee?
I used to think, before I knew,
The prayer not said unless we do.
And did Thy Mother at the night

(Continued on page 76)

Kiss Thee, and fold the clothes in right?
And didst Thou feel quite good in bed,
Kissed, and sweet, and Thy prayers said?

Thou canst not have forgotten all
That it feels like to be small:
And Thou know'st I cannot pray
To Thee in my father's way—
When Thou wast so little, say,
Couldst Thou talk Thy Father's way?—
So, a little Child, come down
And hear a child's tongue like Thy own;
Take me by the hand and walk,
And listen to my baby-talk.
To Thy Father show my prayer
(He will look, Thou art so fair),
And say: "O Father, I, Thy Son,
Bring the prayer of a little one."
And He will smile, that children's tongue
Has not changed since Thou wast young!

—FRANCIS THOMPSON
(1859-1907)

A SELECTION
OF
CHRISTMAS CAROLS

ILLUMINATED MANUSCRIPT
(*XVth Century*)

ANGELS WE HAVE HEARD

Angels we have heard on high,
　　Sweetly singing o'er our plains,
And the mountains in reply
Echoing their joyous strains.
Gloria in excelsis Deo, Gloria in excelsis Deo.

In the fields, beside their sheep,
Shepherds watching thro' the night,
Hear, amid the silence deep,
Those sweet voices, clear and bright.
Gloria in excelsis Deo, Gloria in excelsis Deo.

Joyful hearts with one accord,
Spread the tidings far and wide:
Born to us is Christ the Lord,
At this happy Christmas tide.
Gloria in excelsis Deo, Gloria in excelsis Deo.

—Anonymous

O COME, ALL YE FAITHFUL

O come, all ye faithful, joyful and triumphant,
    O come ye, O come ye to Bethlehem;
Come and behold Him, born the King of angels;
O come, let us adore Him, O come, let us adore Him,
O come, let us adore Him, Christ the Lord.

Lo, humble shepherds, hasting to His cradle,
Leaving their flocks in the fields, draw near.
We, too, with gladness, thither bend our footsteps,
O come, let us adore Him, O come, let us adore Him,
O come, let us adore Him, Christ the Lord.

Sing, choirs of angels, sing in exultation,
Sing, all ye citizens of heav'n above:
"Glory to God in the highest";
O come, let us adore Him, O come, let us adore Him,
O come, let us adore Him, Christ the Lord.

—Anonymous, *about* 1700

WATCHMAN, TELL US OF THE NIGHT

Watchman, tell us of the night,
    What its signs of promise are.
Traveler, o'er yon mountain's height
  See that glory-beaming star.
Watchman, doth its beauteous ray
  Aught of hope or joy foretell?
Traveler, yes, it brings the day,
  Promised day of Israel.

Watchman, tell us of the night,
  Higher yet that star ascends.
Traveler, blessedness and light,
  Peace and truth its course'portends.
Watchman, will its beams alone
  Gild the spot that gave them birth?
Traveler, ages are its own,
  See! it bursts o'er all the earth.

Watchman, tell us of the night,
  For the morning seems to dawn.
Traveler, darkness takes its flight,
  Doubt and terror are withdrawn.
Watchman, let thy wanderings cease,
  Hie thee to thy quiet home.
Traveler, lo! the Prince of Peace,
  Lo! the Son of God is come!

—JOHN BOWRING, 1825

YE SHEPHERD PLAINS OF BETHLEHEM

Ye shepherd plains of Bethlehem,
  That rest in silence long,
Break forth your Christmas echoes, till
  Men hear the angels' song.

Ye shadowed homes in lands oppressed
  By centuries of wrong,
Let heavenly gladness enter in
  For, hark, the angels' song.

All ye who hear from far and near,
  The Christmas joy prolong;
Learn in the fulness of your hearts
  To sing the angels' song.

Ye wider plains of neighbor lands,
  Ye hills and mountains strong,
Take up the sound and everywhere
  Repeat the angels' song.

Ye busy towns and cities vast,
  With all your hurried throng,
Calm now your noise and tumult, while
  Ye learn the angels' song.

—WILLIAM MERRIAM CRANE

THANK WE NOW THE LORD OF HEAV'N

Thank we now the Lord of heav'n
    For the day-spring He has giv'n;
For the light of truth and grace
Shining from the Master's face.
Still that light is shining on:
Still the Holy Child is born
Every blessed Christmas morn.

Still His words of truth and grace
In a holier world we trace;
Still the angels' song is heard:
"Glory be to God on high."
Sing, ye angels from the sky;
Mortals raise the glad refrain,
"Peace on earth, good will to men!"

—HENRY WARBURTON HAWKES

WE THREE KINGS OF ORIENT ARE

We three kings of Orient are;
    Bearing gifts we traverse afar
Field and fountain, moor and mountain,
Following yonder star.

Refrain:

O star of wonder, star of might, star, with royal beauty bright,
Westward leading, still proceeding, guide us to thy perfect light.

Born a King on Bethlehem's plain,
Gold I bring, to crown Him again,
King forever, ceasing never,
Over us all to reign.

Refrain

Frankincense to offer have I,
Incense owns a Deity nigh.
Prayer and praising, all men raising,
Worship God most high.

Refrain

Myrrh is mine, its bitter perfume
Breathes a life of gathering gloom;
Sorrowing, sighing, bleeding, dying,
Sealed in the stone-cold tomb.

Refrain

See Him now in power arise,
Mighty through His sacrifice.
Alleluia! Alleluia!
Echo it, earth and skies.

Refrain

—JOHN H. HOPKINS, JR., 1857

I HEARD THE BELLS ON CHRISTMAS DAY

I heard the bells on Christmas day
  Their old familiar carols play,
And wild and sweet the words repeat
Of "Peace on earth, good will to men!"

And thought how, as the day had come,
The belfries of all Christendom
Had rolled along th' unbroken song,
Of "Peace on earth, good will to men!"

And in despair I bowed my head;
"There is no peace on earth," I said,
"For hate is strong and mocks the song
Of peace on earth, good will to men!"

Then pealed the bells more loud and deep:
"God is not dead; nor doth He sleep!
The wrong shall fail, the right prevail,
With peace on earth, good will to men!"

—HENRY WADSWORTH LONGFELLOW

WHAT MEANS THIS GLORY ROUND OUR FEET?

What means this glory round our feet,"
   The magi mused, "more bright than morn?"
And voices chanted clear and sweet,
   "Today the Prince of Peace is born."

"What means that star," the shepherds said,
   "That brightens through the rocky glen?"
And angels, answ'ring overhead,
   Sang, "Peace on earth, good will to men."

All round about our feet shall shine
   A light like that the wise men saw,
If we our loving wills incline
   To that sweet life which is the law.

So shall we learn to understand
   The simple faith of shepherds then,
And clasping kindly hand in hand,
   Sing, "Peace on earth, good will to men."

And they who to their childhood cling,
   And keep at eve the faith of morn,
Shall daily hear the angels sing,
   "Today the Prince of Peace is born."

—James Russell Lowell, 1866

SILENT NIGHT

Silent night! peaceful night!
　　All things sleep, shepherds keep
Watch on Bethlehem's silent hill,
And unseen, while all is still,
Angels watch above, angels watch above.

Bright the star shines afar,
Guiding travelers on their way,
Who their gold and incense bring,
Offerings to the promised King,
Child of David's line, Child of David's line.

Light around! joyous sound!
Angel voices wake the air;
"Glory be to God in heaven;
Peace on earth to you is given;
Christ, the Saviour is come, Christ, the Saviour, is come!"

—JOSEPH MOHR, 1818
Translation Anonymous

GOOD CHRISTIAN MEN

G ood Christian men, rejoice with heart, and soul, and voice;
    Give ye heed to what we say: Jesus Christ is born today:
Ox and ass before Him bow, He is in the manger now.
Christ is born today! Christ is born today!

Good Christian men, rejoice with heart, and soul, and voice;
Tidings hear of fullest bliss: Jesus Christ was born for this:
Unto you both way and door—life and light for evermore.
Christ was born for this! Christ was born for this!

Good Christian men, rejoice with heart, and soul, and voice;
Lo, the message which ye crave: Jesus Christ was born to save.
Born to bring to men good will, fainting hearts with hope to fill.
Christ was born to save! Christ was born to save!

—Translation by JOHN M. NEALE, 1853

IT CAME UPON THE MIDNIGHT CLEAR

It came upon the midnight clear,
 That glorious song of old,
From angels bending near the earth,
 To touch their harps of gold;
"Peace on the earth, good will to men,
 From heav'n's all-gracious King."
The world in solemn stillness lay
 To hear the angels sing.

Still thro' the cloven skies they come,
 With peaceful wings unfurled;
And still their heavenly music floats
 O'er all the weary world:
Above its sad and lowly plains
 They bend on hovering wing,
And ever o'er its Babel sounds
 The blessed angels sing.

But with the woes of sin and strife
 The world has suffered long;
Beneath the angel-strain have rolled
 Two thousand years of wrong;
And man, at war with man, hears not
 The love song which they bring;
O hush the noise, ye men of strife,
 And hear the angels sing!

And ye, beneath life's crushing load
 Whose forms are bending low,
Who toil along the climbing way,
 With painful steps and slow—
Look now; for glad and golden hours
 Come swiftly on the wing:
O rest beside the weary road,
 And hear the angels sing!

—EDMUND HAMILTON SEARS, 1849

WHILE SHEPHERDS WATCHED
THEIR FLOCKS BY NIGHT

While shepherds watched their flocks by night,
    All seated on the ground,
The angel of the Lord came down,
And glory shone around, and glory shone around.

"To you, in David's town this day,
Is born of David's line,
The Saviour, who is Christ, the Lord,
And this shall be the sign: and this shall be the sign:

"The heav'nly babe you there shall find
To human view displayed,
All meanly wrapped in swathing bands,
And in a manger laid. And in a manger laid."

Thus spake the seraph—and forthwith
Appeared a shining throng
Of angels, praising God, who thus
Addressed their joyful song; addressed their joyful song;

"All glory be to God on high,
And to the earth be peace;
Good will henceforth from heaven to men
Begin, and never cease! Begin and never cease!"

—NAHUM TATE
(1652-1715)

THE FIRST NOWELL

The first Nowell the angel did say
Was to certain poor shepherds, in fields as they lay,
In fields where they lay keeping their sheep.
On a cold winter's night that was so deep.

Refrain:

Nowell, Nowell, Nowell, Nowell, born is the King of Israel.

They lookéd up and saw a star,
Shining in the east beyond them far,
And to the earth it gave great light,
And so it continued both day and night.

Refrain

And by the light of that same star,
Three wise men came from country far;
To seek for a king was their intent,
And to follow the star wherever it went.

Refrain

This star drew nigh to the northwest,
O'er Bethlehem it took its rest,
And there it did both stop and stay,
Right o'er the place where Jesus lay.

Refrain

Then did they know assuredly,
Within that house the King did lie,
One entered in then for to see,
And found the Babe in poverty.

Refrain

Then entered in those wise men three,
Most reverently upon their knee,
And offered there, in His presence,
Both gold, and myrrh, and frankincense.

Refrain

—TRADITIONAL

JOY TO THE WORLD

Joy to the world! the Lord is come:
   Let earth receive her King;
Let every heart prepare Him room,
   And heaven and nature sing, and heaven and nature sing.

Joy to the earth! the Saviour reigns:
   Let men their songs employ,
While fields and floods, rocks, hills, and plains
   Repeat the sounding joy, repeat the sounding joy.

No more let sins and sorrows grow,
   Nor thorns infest the ground;
He comes to make His blessings flow
   As far as sin is found, as far as sin is found.

He rules the world with truth and grace,
   And makes the nations prove
The glories of His righteousness,
   And wonders of His love, and wonders of His love.

—ISAAC WATTS, 1719

IN THE LONELY MIDNIGHT

In the lonely midnight, on the wintry hill,
    Shepherds heard the angels singing, "Peace, good will."
Listen, O ye weary, to the angels' song,
Unto you the tidings of great joy belong.

Tho' in David's city angels sing no more,
Love makes angel music on earth's darkest shore;
Tho' no heav'nly glory meet your wond'ring eyes,
Love can make your dwelling bright as paradise.

Tho' the Child of Mary, sent from heav'n on high,
In His manger cradle may no longer lie,
Love is king forever, tho' the proud world scorn;
If you truly seek Him, Christ your King is born.

                    —THEODORE CHICKERING WILLIAMS

INDEX BY TITLES

A Selection of Christmas Carols